# I Wonder Why
# Camels
# Have Humps

and other questions about animals

**Anita Ganeri**

KINGFISHER
NEW YORK

**KINGFISHER**
LONDON & NEW YORK

Copyright © 1993 by Kingfisher
Published in the United States by Kingfisher,
175 Fifth Ave., New York, NY 10010
Kingfisher is an imprint of Macmillan Children's Books, London.
All rights reserved.

Distributed in the U.S. by Macmillan,
175 Fifth Ave., New York, NY 10010
Distributed in Canada by H.B. Fenn and Company Ltd.,
34 Nixon Road, Bolton, Ontario L7E 1W2

LIBRARY OF CONGRESS CATALOGING-IN-PUBLICATION DATA
Ganeri, Anita.
    I wonder why camels have humps and other
questions about animals/by Anita Ganeri.
    p. cm.
        Includes index.
        Summary: Addresses such questions about animals as why camels
have humps, how bats see in the dark, and why birds have feathers.
        1. Animals—Miscellanea—Juvenile literature.
    [1. Animals—Habits and behavior.—2. Questions
    and answers.] I Title.
    QL49.G2426 1993
    591—dc20 92-44260 CIP AC

ISBN: 978-0-7534-5660-6

Kingfisher books are available for special promotions and premiums.
For details contact: Special Markets Department, Macmillan,
175 Fifth Avenue, New York, NY 10010.

For more information, please visit www.kingfisherpublications.com

First published in hardcover in 1993; first published
in paperback in 1997; first published in this format in 2003

Printed in Taiwan
9 8 7 6

6TR/0110/SHENS/UNIV(FR)/126.MA/F

*Series editor:* Jackie Gaff
*Series designer:* David West
    Children's Books
*Consultant:* Michael Chinery
*Illustrations:* Steven Holmes
    (Eunice McMullen);Tony
    Kenyon (B. L. Kearley)
    all cartoons

# CONTENTS

● Female Queen Alexandra's birdwings are the world's biggest butterflies. Their wings are almost as big as this page!

● The blue whale is so long that eight elephants could stand along its back.

Giraffe
18 feet (5.5 m)
tall

Elephant
11 feet (3.5 m)
tall — 7 tons

Ostrich
8 feet (2.5 m) tall

● The giraffe is the tallest land animal. With its long neck, it can reach as high as a two-story house.

● The mighty African elephant is almost three times as tall as you are. It can weigh as much as seven cars.

● The ostrich is the world's tallest and heaviest bird. It's as tall as a bus!

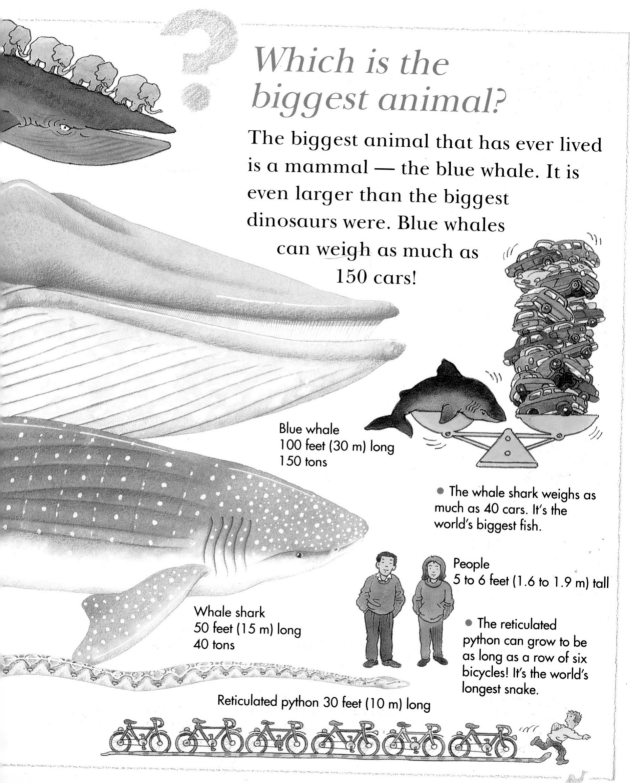

# Which is the biggest animal?

The biggest animal that has ever lived is a mammal — the blue whale. It is even larger than the biggest dinosaurs were. Blue whales can weigh as much as 150 cars!

Blue whale
100 feet (30 m) long
150 tons

● The whale shark weighs as much as 40 cars. It's the world's biggest fish.

People
5 to 6 feet (1.6 to 1.9 m) tall

Whale shark
50 feet (15 m) long
40 tons

● The reticulated python can grow to be as long as a row of six bicycles! It's the world's longest snake.

Reticulated python 30 feet (10 m) long

# What's the difference between sharks and dolphins?

Although sharks and dolphins look alike, they belong to two very different animal groups. Sharks are a kind of fish, but dolphins are members of another group, the mammals.

● You don't look anything like a dolphin, but you are a mammal, too!

● If an animal breathes air through lungs, and its babies feed on their mother's milk, it's a mammal. Most mammals have some fur or hair on their bodies.

Lungs

● If an animal has feathers and hatches out of a hard-shelled egg, it's a bird. All birds have wings, and most of them can fly.

● If an animal has six legs and three parts to its body, it's an insect. There are more kinds of insect in the world than all the other kinds of animal put together.

Abdomen

Head

Thorax

● If an animal has damp slimy skin, and is born in water but lives much of its life on land, it's an amphibian. Baby amphibians hatch out of jellylike eggs.

● If an animal has a dry scaly skin and is born on land, it's a reptile. Most reptiles lay eggs with leathery skins.

Scaly skin

Fin

Gill

● If an animal lives in water, breathes through gills, and uses fins to move, it's a fish. Most fish lay jellylike eggs that hatch into baby fish.

# What's the difference between frogs and toads?

Frogs usually have smooth skin and long legs for leaping. Most toads have lumpy skin and move their short thick bodies about by crawling.

Toad

Frog

# ...and alligators and crocodiles?

Crocodiles have longer, more pointed snouts than alligators. Crocodiles also have one very large tooth sticking up on each side when they close their mouths.

- Frogs and toads are both amphibians.

- Alligators and crocodiles are reptiles.

Crocodile

Alligator

# ...and between monkeys and apes?

The big difference between these animals is that monkeys have long tails, but apes don't have tails at all. There are lots of different kinds of monkey, but the only apes are gorillas, orangutans, chimpanzees, and gibbons.

Spider monkey

Orangutan (ape)

● Monkeys and apes are mammals

● A woodlouse looks like it's an insect, but it isn't — it has too many legs! This creepy-crawly is related to crabs and lobsters.

● Rabbits and hares are both mammals.

# ...and rabbits and hares?

Hares have longer legs and ears than rabbits. Their whiskers are longer, too.

# Why do animals have skeletons inside their bodies?

Not all animals have skeletons, but most large ones do. This is because the bigger an animal is, the more it needs a strong sturdy framework to hold its body together and carry its weight. Skeletons also protect soft inside parts, like brains and hearts.

Backbone

● Animals without backbones are called invertebrates. Insects, spiders, snails, worms, jellyfish, shrimps, and crabs are all invertebrates.

Backbone

● Animals with backbones are called vertebrates. Fish are vertebrates, and so are amphibians, reptiles, birds, and mammals.

- Most animals' skeletons are made of bone, but a shark's skeleton is made of gristle. This isn't as hard as bone, but it's still tough. You have some in your nose.

- Insects, spiders, scorpions, centipedes, and millipedes all have tough exoskeletons.

Millipede

- Lobsters, crabs, and some beetles have really tough exoskeletons that work like armor to protect them from attack.

- Squid are the biggest kind of invertebrate. The longest one ever found measured more than 55 feet (17 m) from its head to the tip of its tentacles — longer than eight scuba divers!

- To grow larger, an animal has to break out of its old exoskeleton and grow a new one.

# Which animals have skeletons on the outside?

Most smaller animals have tough skins called exoskeletons. These outside skeletons do the same job as inside ones. They protect and support the animals' soft bodies.

# Why do camels have humps?

A camel's hump is its own built-in food cupboard. By living off the fat stored in its hump, a camel can go for as long as two weeks without eating. Camels need their humps because they live in deserts, where food and water are hard to find.

# Why do elephants have trunks?

An elephant's trunk is a helpful tool. It can be used to pull down leaves and branches to eat. It also makes a good hose — elephants can squirt dust or water over themselves to keep cool.

● Elephants say "hello" to friends by shaking trunks with them.

● An elephant's trunk is a bit like a hand. Using its tip, an elephant can pick up something as small as a button.

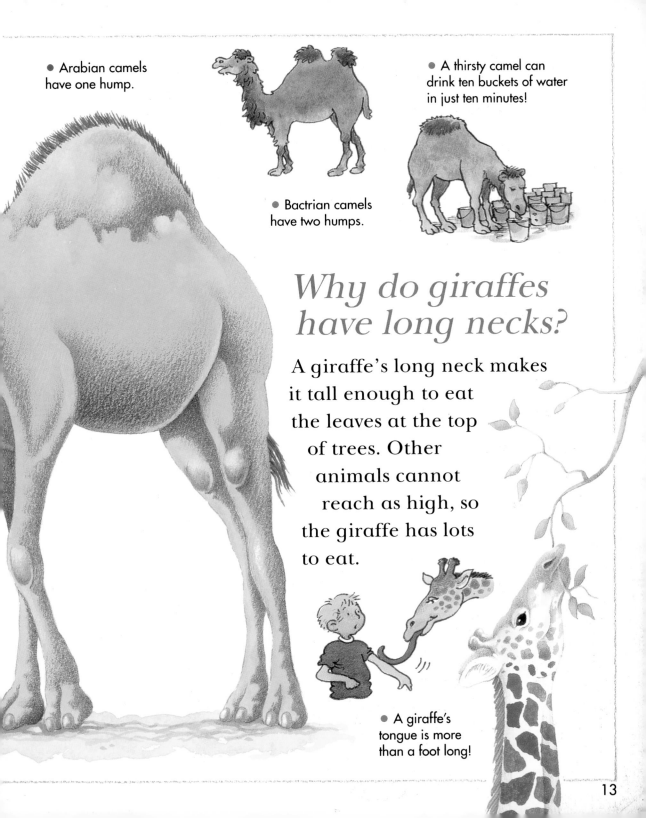

- Arabian camels have one hump.

- Bactrian camels have two humps.

- A thirsty camel can drink ten buckets of water in just ten minutes!

# Why do giraffes have long necks?

A giraffe's long neck makes it tall enough to eat the leaves at the top of trees. Other animals cannot reach as high, so the giraffe has lots to eat.

- A giraffe's tongue is more than a foot long!

# Which bird has eyes in the back of its head?

An owl's eyes aren't really in the back of its head, but at times they might as well be! Owls have such flexible necks that when they want to look backward they swivel their heads right around!

● An owl's huge eyes help it to see at night. This is when most owls fly around, hunting for food.

# How do bats see in the dark?

Bats not only fly at night without bumping into things, they also manage to hunt down juicy insects to eat. Bats can do this even when it's pitch dark, because they use sound, not light, to find their way.

● Bats make lots of very high squeaking sounds as they fly. When these sounds hit objects — such as insects or trees — they bounce off them, back toward the bats. The repeated sounds are called echoes. And bats can tell where things are by listening to them.

● The blue-tongued skink sticks out its big blue tongue to frighten enemies away.

● Starfish don't have heads, but they do have eyes. They are on the ends of their arms.

# Which animals smell with their tongues?

Snakes and lizards don't smell with their noses as we do. Instead, they flick their long tongues in and out. Their tongues pick up smells from the air and the ground, helping them to track down things to eat.

● African elephants have ears as big as bedspreads — the biggest ears in the world. Elephants have very good hearing, but their ears are also useful for keeping cool. They can be flapped like fans, for example.

# Why are zebras striped?

No one knows for sure why zebras have striped coats, but it must help them to see each other so that they can stay together in a herd. There's safety in numbers, of course — especially against hungry lions!

● No two zebras have exactly the same pattern of stripes — just as no two people have exactly the same fingerprints!

● Some things give you spots in front of your eyes, but a herd of galloping zebras would give you stripes! For a lion, it must be even harder to pick which zebra to chase.

# Why do leopards have spots?

A leopard's spots help it to hide among trees and bushes, so it can pounce out and surprise its prey. The light and dark patches in its fur match the patches of sunlight and shadow under the leafy branches.

# Which animal changes color?

Chameleons usually have brownish-green skin, but it only takes them a few minutes to change their color completely!

These strange animals can change color to match things around them, which helps them hide from enemies. Chameleons also change color when angry or frightened.

● The fur of some animals that live in cold countries is brown in summer and white in winter. This makes it harder to see the animals when snow covers the ground.

# Why are flamingos pink?

Flamingos take their pink color from their favorite food — shrimps! If these leggy birds don't get enough shrimps to eat, they turn a dull gray.

# Why do birds have feathers?

Feathers keep birds warm. They also help them to fly, by giving their wings and bodies a special sleek shape.

Each kind of bird has feathers of a different color and pattern. Males are often brighter than females — their good looks help them to attract a mate!

● Birds' fluffy down feathers trap warm air next to their skin just as a comforter keeps you warm in bed.

● Hummingbirds are among the world's smallest birds. The bee hummingbird lays its eggs in a nest the size of a walnut.

# Which bird can fly backward?

Hummingbirds are the helicopters of the bird world. They can fly in all directions — backward, forward, sideways, up and down. They can even hover on one spot.

- Birds can fly by flapping their wings up and down, or by gliding on still, outstretched wings.

# Why can't penguins fly?

Penguins can't fly because their wings are too small to keep their heavy bodies up in the air. But penguins are very good swimmers and divers. They use their wings as paddles in the water.

- Most birds can fold their wings up close to their bodies, but penguins can't. They always hold their wings stiffly out to the side.

- Ostriches are too big to fly, but they can run at twice the speed of the fastest Olympic runners.

# Which frogs can fly?

Tree frogs can climb trees, and some kinds can even glide from one tree to another! These unusual frogs have big feet with long webbed toes. When they spread their toes out, the webs of skin between them act like parachutes and help the frogs to glide.

● Flying fish don't really fly. Instead, they leap out of the sea and then spread out extra-long fins which help them to glide. They do this to escape their enemies.

● The paradise flying snake can glide from tree to tree. To climb them, it grips the bark with its scaly underside.

# Which animals can walk upside down?

Geckos are small lizards, and some can walk upside down! They have special toes that help them hold on.

● The ridges on a gecko's toes are covered in tiny bristles, each of which ends in a tiny sucker pad.

● Unlike most fish, mudskippers can get oxygen from air as well as water. This allows them to stay alive out of the water.

# Which fish can climb trees?

The last place you'd expect to see a fish is up a tree — but then the mudskipper is a very odd fish! It climbs with its leglike fins, clinging on with a sort of suction cup on its belly.

# How high can a kangaroo hop?

Believe it or not, big kangaroos can hop right over your head! As far as we know, the highest a kangaroo has ever jumped is about 10 feet (3 m) — more than twice as high as you are tall. Their big, strong back legs help kangaroos to be such good high jumpers.

● For their size, fleas are the world's best high jumpers. They can jump over 100 times their own height.

● By hopping in giant leaps, big kangaroos can move nearly as fast as racehorses!

# How fast can a cheetah run?

● Cheetahs use their sharp claws to grip and push against the ground as they race along. Olympic runners have spikes on their shoes for the same reason.

A hungry cheetah can sprint faster than 60 miles per hour (100 km/h) when chasing something to eat. But running this fast soon wears it out, and it has to stop to get its breath back.

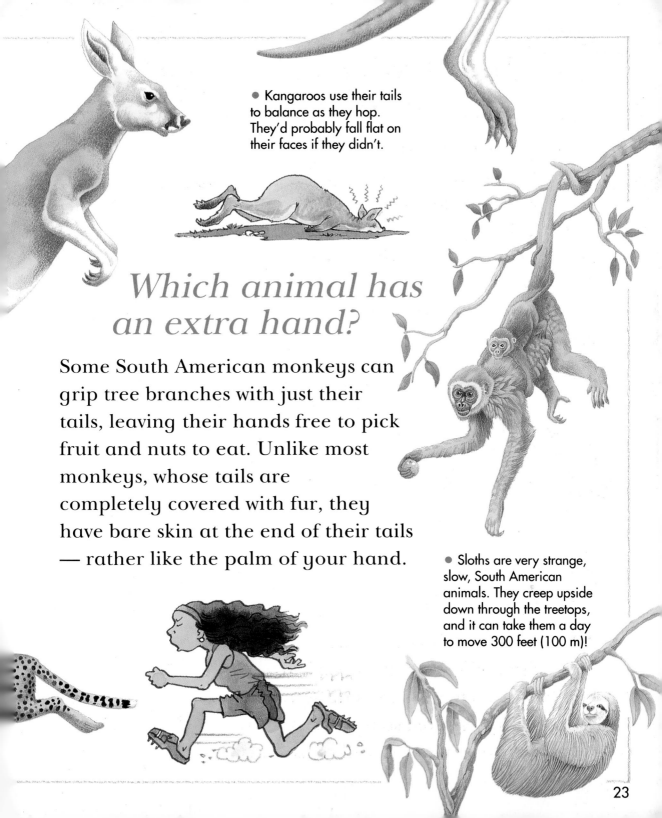

● Kangaroos use their tails to balance as they hop. They'd probably fall flat on their faces if they didn't.

# Which animal has an extra hand?

Some South American monkeys can grip tree branches with just their tails, leaving their hands free to pick fruit and nuts to eat. Unlike most monkeys, whose tails are completely covered with fur, they have bare skin at the end of their tails — rather like the palm of your hand.

● Sloths are very strange, slow, South American animals. They creep upside down through the treetops, and it can take them a day to move 300 feet (100 m)!

# How many ants can an anteater eat?

On a good day, a giant anteater eats an amazing 30,000 ants! It can scoop up as many as 500 with each flick of its long sticky tongue. Anteaters don't munch their food because they don't have any teeth. They swallow the ants whole.

● Giant anteaters have to walk on the knuckles of their front feet because their claws are so long and sharp. They use these claws to rip ant hills apart.

● Birds that feed on fish often have long sharp beaks. The anhinga uses its beak to spear fish.

● Bears tear bees' nests apart to get at the honey inside. They don't seem to mind getting stung.

# Which animal uses its finger as a fork?

A strange monkeylike animal called an aye-aye has one finger much longer than the others on each hand. It uses these spindly fingers to poke under tree bark for grubs and insects to eat. Then it skewers them, using its fingers as you would use a fork.

● Aye-ayes only live on the island of Madagascar, off the east coast of Africa.

# Which is the greediest animal?

For its size, the tiny Etruscan shrew has the world's biggest appetite. It hardly ever stops eating! By the time it's full grown, it has to eat three times its own weight in food each day.

● An adult Etruscan shrew weighs less than a sugar lump.

# Which animals shoot their food?

If an archer fish spots an insect sitting on a plant above the water, it shoots it — not with an arrow or a bullet, of course, but with a jet of water squirted from its mouth. The insect falls into the water and the fish gobbles it up.

- The bolas spider swings a thread with a sticky blob at the end to catch insects. A bolas is a kind of lasso used by South American cowboys.

- The archer fish is a good shot. It can hit an insect up to 10 feet (3 m) away from it.

- The sound of the pistol shrimp's big left pincer snapping shut sends shock waves through the water, stunning small fish and making them easier to catch.

# Which animals drink blood?

The world's most bloodthirsty animals are vampire bats, mosquitoes, and some kinds of leech. Vampire bats don't usually drink people's blood, but mosquitoes and leeches aren't so choosy!

● Leeches swell up as they feed. Only some kinds suck blood.

# Which birds use fish bait?

Green herons use insects and feathers as bait to catch fish. The heron drops its bait in the water, then waits for a fish to spot it. The fish thinks it has found a tasty snack, but ends up as the heron's meal instead!

# Why do opossums play dead?

If the Virginia opossum is attacked, it sometimes tries to fool its enemy into leaving it alone by playing dead. Its eyes go glassy, and it lies quite still with its tongue hanging out. It's more usual — and safer — for an opossum to run away, though, or climb a tree!

● Grass snakes try to escape their enemies by playing dead, too.

# Which is the smelliest animal?

The skunk is a very smelly creature. If an enemy makes the mistake of getting too close, the skunk sprays it with a stinking oily liquid. The terrible smell can last for days!

# Which is the prickliest animal?

Porcupines are pricklier than any pincushion. Their backs are covered in hundreds of long sharp quills, with barbs like fishhooks on the ends.

● If a porcupine is attacked, it raises and spreads its quills, rattling them as a warning. Then it rushes backward toward its enemy.

● Some crabs have their own bodyguards. They carry a sea anemone in each claw so that the anemones' tentacles can sting any enemies that get too close.

● Porcupine fish blow themselves up into prickly balls when enemies attack.

# Do animals kill people?

Many animals are dangerous if they are hunting for food or if something frightens them. But very few animals will attack people for no reason.

● Tigers usually hunt large animals such as deer. But if a tiger is too sick to hunt, it may attack people instead.

● The tiny arrow-poison frogs of South America ooze deadly poison from their brightly colored skin.

# Are all snakes poisonous?

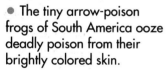

Not all snakes are poisonous. And only a few have poison strong enough to kill people. The most deadly are sea snakes, cobras, vipers, and rattlesnakes.

● Some of the biggest snakes aren't poisonous. They squeeze their victims to death.

# Are all sharks dangerous?

Many sharks are meat-eaters, but very few will attack people. Although millions of people swim in areas where there are sharks, there are fewer than 1,000 shark attacks a year.

● The great white shark sometimes attacks swimmers.

● Some of the great white shark's teeth are longer than your fingers!

● Cobras have poison fangs.

● Sharkskin is so rough that it was once used as sandpaper.

● Sharks can grow a new set of teeth every two weeks.

# Index